essentials

Speaking in Public

7

'10

Time-saving books that teach specific skills to busy people, focusing on what really matters; the things that make a difference – the *essentials*. Other books in the series include:

Making Great Presentations

Writing Good Reports

Responding to Stress

Succeeding at Interviews

Solving Problems

Hiring People

Getting Started on the Internet

Writing Great Copy

Making the Best Man's Speech

Feeling Good for No Reason

Making the Most of Your Time

For full details please send for a free copy of the latest catalogue. See back cover for address.

The things that really matter about

Speaking
in Public

John Bowden

ESSENTIALS

Published in 1999 by
How To Books Ltd, 3 Newtec Place,
Magdalen Road, Oxford OX4 1RE, United Kingdom
Tel: (01865) 793806   Fax: (01865) 248780
email: info@howtobooks.co.uk
www.howtobooks.co.uk

British Library Cataloguing in Publication Data.
A catalogue record for this book is available from
the British Library.

Edited by David Venner
Cover design by Shireen Nathoo Design
Produced for How To Books by Deer Park Productions
Typeset by PDQ Typesetting, Newcastle-under-Lyme, Staffordshire
Printed and bound in Great Britain

NOTE: The material contained in this book is set out in good faith for general guidance and no liability can be accepted for loss or expense incurred
as a result of relying in particular circumstances on
statements made in the book. Laws and regulations are complex
and liable to change, and readers should check the current position
with the relevant authorities before making personal arrangements.

ESSENTIALS *is an imprint of*
How To Books

Contents

Preface

In a recent survey about fears, which do you suppose people were more afraid of – speaking in public or dying? That's right. More people feared the prospect of having to stand up and speak to an audience than feared dying.

What is the key to explaining this irrational fear? It is that we suddenly feel very exposed. It's rather like having your outer protective shell peeled off – there is nothing left to hide behind. It's far worse than stage fright because it's the real you out there, not just an actor playing a part.

Have you ever been to a conference or attended a lecture given by a 'big name' and found yourself disappointed and bored because the speaker failed to communicate? On other occasions, have you ever been pleasantly surprised and excited by an 'unknown' who came over as extremely self-confident, amusing and informative?

So what makes one person totally absorbing and another excruciatingly boring? That's the 64,000 euro question. And that's what this book is all about – learning how to make yourself impressive and consistently getting what you want out of your speeches.

Proficiency in speaking is not a gift – it can be learnt. This is fact, not fancy. By getting back to basics, by concentrating on the essentials, and by learning about the things that really matter, you can and will dramatically improve your effectiveness as a public speaker.

John Bowden

1 Learning the Essentials

Public speakers are vested with tremendous credibility and support when they ascend the platform. It's the fault of the speaker, not the audience, when things go wrong.

things that really matter

1 **SETTING YOUR PRINCIPAL OBJECTIVE**

2 **KNOWING YOUR AUDIENCE**

3 **GETTING WHAT YOU WANT OUT OF YOUR SPEECH**

Establishing your main objective is the most important part of speech preparation. Surprisingly, it is also the one most often overlooked. You must first be absolutely sure *why* you are going to speak. Only then can you even begin to think about what you are going to say and how you are going to say it.

Whether you're going to be speaking at a Sales Conference, Product Launch, Rotary Lunch, Ladies' Night, Bar Mitzvah, or at any other function, always begin by establishing your single, principal objective. What precisely do you want to *achieve*? In other words, ask yourself: 'What do I want this audience to *do* or *think* or *feel* differently as a result of my speech?'

Once you are absolutely clear about your **principal objective**, find out as much as you can about **your audience**. Only then can you decide how you can best achieve **your principal objective** with **this particular audience**.

IS THIS YOU?

• *I have been disappointed in my previous efforts at public speaking and want to improve.* • *I am moving into a new job which requires me to make speeches and presentations. Quite simply, I don't know where to begin.* • *I need to make a one-off speech. I'm a specialist in my field, but an inexperienced public speaker.* • *I've been a public speaker for years. I am quite confident but feel it's time to add a little polish to my act.* • *With some audiences my speeches seem to go down well, with others they just go down. Don't ask me why.*

① SETTING YOUR PRINCIPAL OBJECTIVE

Every time you speak in public you should have a **single, overriding objective**. It may be:

- the transfer of skills to an audience
- the initiation of immediate action
- the provocation of their emotions
- the interactions among them
- or the appreciation of their potential.

A presentation on time management skills should improve productivity. A lecture on sales techniques should lead to improved sales closing rates. A talk embracing a message of hope should help people to resolve their own problems.

An objective is not what you intend to say, it is what you intend to achieve.

To make a speech without any regard as to how it will improve your audience's condition is the equivalent of a salesperson making sales calls and considering that a job well done. Sales calls are no more than a means to an end. Salespeople should have the principal objective of bringing in new business. Speeches are no more than a means to an end. Speakers should have the principal objective of improving the condition of their audience by achieving or exceeding some planned outcome.

If you don't leave the audience in a better condition than it was before you spoke, then there is no point in having spoken at all.

The mere act of exploring, understanding and clarifying your precise objective will add enormous value to your contribution. The status quo is not the desire or there would be no need for a speech. What **outcome** do you want? What **changes** do you require in the audience's **attitude** and **behaviour**? What **value** can you **add**? This must always be considered in terms of some **output**, some **result**, some **bettered position**. By what standard will you judge success?

Simplify your principal objective to one sentence, for example: 'If they leave with this [specific skill, ability, technique, attitude, awareness], my objective will have been achieved'.

The more **concrete** and **specific** you make this principal objective, the more accurately you will be able to gauge the **effectiveness** of your speech.

A speech without an objective is like a car without an engine ... The only way it can go is downhill.

 KNOWING YOUR AUDIENCE

The key to effective public speaking is **relevance**. As Ronald Reagan so aptly put it, about the tough economic times that characterised the period of his presidency, 'Recession is when your neighbour loses his job. Depression is when you lose yours.'

Relevance generates interest and attention; irrelevance generates apathy and boredom.

As a child listening to your mother tell you about all those starving children in Africa who would love to eat your plate of greens, you weren't too concerned about poverty. But after six months without a job, and relying on that fortnightly giro, poverty gets your attention. Relevance makes the difference.

If you are addressing an audience of fishermen in Scotland, they will not warm to a story set in a gay disco in San Francisco. Yet if you are speaking to an audience of amateur cricketers, a blow by blow account of a number eleven batsman's final over heroics will bowl them over. Relevance makes the difference.

If you want to gain an audience's attention you must not speak to them as people in general. You need to focus specifically on **what matters to them**. Here are three helpful ways you can find out about the composition, knowledge, expectations and needs of an audience.

- Think carefully over what you already know about this particular audience and situation.

- Consult with other individuals or groups who have addressed the same audience.

- Either speak directly with selected audience members or form your impressions indirectly by consulting with their colleagues.

Use your findings to help pitch the speech at the **right level** and to **customise your remarks** to encourage their feelings and reactions. Keep the group attitude in mind throughout and **personalise** even the most remote issue so they can see a connection between themselves and it. If people can see how your subject matter relates to them, they will remain interested. You can also bring in specific **comments** and **observations** at various junctures: 'From what you've told me...'. 'Those of you I've spoken to recently seem to think...'.

All your witty observations, amusing anecdotes and profound insights into the state of the world must be meaningful and relevant to your audience.

Even if you cannot find out much about an audience before you speak, try to **imagine** what they are like. It is better than trying to address rows of vacant faces. Get a bit of background information about them through your opening comments: 'My name is Pat Smith and I'm the chairman of Slowcoach Buses. I understand some of you are engineers and some are in sales. Would you raise your hand if you're from engineering..., thank you. And if you're from sales..., thank you. And if you're not sure where you're from..., thank you!'

A speech which is perceived as audience-friendly will always go down better than one that is introspective.

 GETTING WHAT YOU WANT OUT OF YOUR SPEECH

The first step, then, is to decide precisely what outcome you are seeking. The second is to find out as much as you can about your audience. The vital third step **reverses** the point of view, using your findings to focus on what is most likely to move this audience to do what you want them to do.

How can you achieve this outcome with this audience? The answer is to be outcome-centred as you plan your speech and audience-centred as you deliver it.

Your principal objective remains paramount. Audience orientation creates a willingness to listen to messages designed to achieve this desired outcome. Confuse them at your peril. Tell the audience what you need to in order to achieve the desired outcome, but tell them this in a way that makes them feel at ease.

You will not motivate, inform, persuade or entertain if an audience feels uncomfortable. External surroundings are important, but the way people feel internally is critical. You can help put any audience at ease, and thereby make them more receptive to your message, by doing four things:

Treat them with respect: Adults make their own decisions. It's always permissible to present options and even challenge assumptions, but it's never a good idea to presume your alternative is the best for everyone. Audiences are no different from you, except that you'll usually be speaking and they'll usually be listening, if you let them.

- **Do not** include stories or exercises simply to make yourself look good. Each component of your speech should be included to help you achieve your principal objective, not to show what a wonderful person you are.

- **Do not** demand participation in any activity that even one person could find demeaning and uncomfortable. Ask for volunteers.

- **Do not** talk down to your audience.

Never overestimate your audience's knowledge; never underestimate its intelligence.

Inject humour into your speech: People are always relaxed by humour, but since most humour is based upon someone else's discomfort, it is often safer to be self-effacing. People will commiserate and empathise ('Been there; done that; got the tee-shirt'). They will identify not merely with your situation, but with your ensuing message.

You do not need to be a stand-up comedian, indeed you should not be. But you must allow the **humorous** side of your personality to shine through. Some of us are naturally witty. But most of us are not. If you cannot tell jokes, then recall amusing personal anecdotes. They always go down well provided they are used in context and the point of the story is obvious.

A joke or anecdote should not be told in isolation. It should arise naturally from whatever preceded it and its punchline should allow you to embark into your next topic. Try to choose gags and stories that have a telling point. In that way, if the tale fails to win a laugh, you can go on talking as if you never meant it to.

This example comes from a talk given to an audience of young mums. Notice how the speaker follows the simple format of: Into joke, Joke, Out of joke. The gag is set up, told, and its punchline allows her to move on, in this case to make a more serious point:

Into joke: Sometimes the walls seem to close in on you. You have got to get out of the house.

Joke: Last week I was walking in the park with my five children when a friendly gardener asked, 'Are all those children yours, or is it a picnic?'. 'They're all mine', I replied – 'and it's certainly no picnic!'

Out of joke: And we all know how difficult life can be at times, don't we...?

If you keep your jokes and anecdotes short, clean and

relevant they will create that all-important ingredient of instant comfort. Try to build humour into every speech you make.

Recognise that there are different learning styles: The best speech preparation embraces the philosophy that people are diverse. Some of us are good listeners, others prefer visual aids. There are those who enjoy group learning, but others prefer solitary absorption. This has important implications for speakers and their preparation and attitude: Use a **range of presentation techniques** and provide **varied sources of input**. For example, use audio-visual aids as well as script; have handouts as well as slides.

Don't outstay your welcome: Don't suffer from the illusion that you can make your speech immortal by making it everlasting. In the Bible, the story of the Creation is told in 400 words (that's about three minutes) and the Ten Commandments are covered in fewer than 300. Yet the latest EU Directive on the importation of caramel products is over 27,000 words long (that would take you over 3½ hours to chew over). Really important things *can* be said quickly, if you get to the point quickly enough.

Get a good ending and a good beginning: and get them close together. Always stop before your audience wants you to. The point of satiation is reached very soon after the peak of popularity.

MAKING WHAT MATTERS WORK FOR YOU

✓ Simplify your principal objective to **one sentence**, for example: 'If customer retention rate improves by 2% by the end of the [next quarter], my objective will have been achieved.'

✓ Remember that every audience is different. Find out as much about **this** audience as you can. Use your findings to help pitch the speech at the right level, and to bring in specific comments and observations which are **meaningful** to them. It is vital to make your speech as relevant for their frame of reference as possible.

✓ You cannot achieve your objective unless your audience feels relaxed, comfortable and 'at home'. Be **outcome-centred** as you prepare your speech but **audience-centred** as you deliver it.

2 Creating Your Speech

The body of any specific speech must express in essence what you know and feel and trust is right to achieve your principal objective.

Don't expect to create a speech in thirty minutes. Select your topic as early as possible, think about it during odd moments, brood over it, sleep on it, dream on it. Every pensive reflection will pay dividends when the time comes to speak your thoughts out loud to your audience.

Most speeches contain far too many facts and figures. Speakers confuse information with communication. In many cases such information overload has the opposite effect. Successful speeches are based on **messages**, not facts.

This chapter shows you how to formulate your most compelling messages and select your most persuasive supporting facts. It then explains how you can **mind map** your speech, create a **cohesive structure** and prepare an audience-friendly script that will engage listeners in the logic of your thoughts. In short, it will show you how to create a dynamic speech.

IS THIS YOU?

• *I like to include plenty of relevant facts, but I find the audience tend to lose interest after a while.*
• *My speeches sound artificial, they just don't sound natural.* • *I try to squeeze in as much information as possible into the limited time available.* • *It's funny, I usually know exactly what I want to say, but I find it extremely difficult to plan the structure of a speech and I find myself rambling on.*
• *I don't know what kind of script to prepare – if any.*

① TAKING A MESSAGE-BASED APPROACH

There is no universal, unchanging way to structure a speech. Formats vary according to several determining factors such as different objectives, audiences, surroundings and speakers. However, one general approach to speech creation always works, regardless of chosen structure: focusing on **messages**, not **facts**.

A fact is something you **know**; a message is the significance of that fact. To tell an audience that a road accident is twice as likely to result in a fatality if the driver is travelling at 35 mph rather than at 30 mph is a fact. To tell them that 'Speed kills' is the associated message. Always base your speech on messages, and support your messages with facts.

Don't tell them everything you know. Tell them everything they need to know.

In order for a message-based approach to be effective, you must be clear about the **context**, **message**, **route map** and **principal objective** of the speech:

The context: Why are you making this speech? What situation has occurred, or is likely to occur, that brings you and your audience together? There must be some significant change or danger or worry or opportunity or you would not be making this speech.

Your success often depends on discovering or implanting some unease, guilt or fear in the audience. For example, you could tell them about business rivals who are now producing improved goods more efficiently.

Nobody is interested in salvation until they have experienced a fear of damnation.

The message. What thought or image do you wish to implant? Boil your message down to one sentence. Put it on a yellow sticky note, and attach it to your computer monitor or desk. In this way you can look at it periodically and make sure you are still on track. Everything you say, do or show should support this message.

If you do not know what message you intend to convey each time you speak, neither will your audience. To tell them a new sales campaign will be initiated next month is not a message, it is a fact. Nor does it relate directly to the needs of the audience. Unless you want people to fidget, fall asleep or walk out, you must have something to say that the audiences will want to hear.

You may care passionately about the new campaign, but your audience won't care less if they don't feel it's **relevant** to them. The essence of a good message is that it will trigger an **emotional** response. You need to find out what *they* really care about and what *their* needs are. You need to sell **benefits** not features.

Your message must be at the heart of the speech. Always remain on-message.

The route map. What ground will you need to cover? What

facts must you discuss so that the audience can have confidence in the veracity of your message? Generally three relevant facts are enough to support any message, often one key fact is adequate. If your message is: 'I am innocent of this crime' and you have the cast-iron alibi that you were at Buckingham Palace, being awarded an OBE, at the time the offence was committed, there is no point in then continuing to argue that you could not possibly have been the perpetrator because you are left-handed or because you have a fear of spiders.

Your facts should provide a **rationale**, a **defence, statistical proof, expert quotes** or **advice**, or anything else you find to uphold your assertions. It is more important to have **quick, defensible proof** than to over-explain every last detail. If necessary, this can be done by means of handouts or at question time.

Include only enough facts – the right facts – to make your message clear.

The principal objective. Put together a speech that focuses on what you want the audience – or perhaps that man sitting in the front row – to **know, think,** or **do. Outcome is all.** There is nothing wrong with getting people fired up briefly but this short term effect is no more than a means to an end.

The vital medium and long-term benefit you must bring is to improve the audience's condition by providing the required skills, techniques and approaches that people continue to demonstrate every day long after you have spoken.

 MIND MAPPING YOUR SPEECH

The theory behind mind mapping is that the brain does not

work as well in a linear or list-like format because it acts on triggers which stimulate new thoughts – it thinks **laterally** rather and vertically.

Rather than starting from the top of a page and working down in conventional sentences or lists, you start from the centre with your message and branch out as dictated by sub-messages and associated ideas and evidence. You have three concentric circles. The smallest circle contains your central message; the middle-sized circle contains your sub-messages; and the largest circle contains your supporting facts.

Many speakers are too ambitious; they try to cover too much ground. Less is more. Have no more than three or four sub-messages. People will not remember more anyway, so don't waste your time.

Here is a possible mind map for an informal ten-minute speech to employees. The intended principal outcome is: 'Our image will be improved and we will achieve a 90% plus approval rating within a year'. Its central message is: 'The more people know us, the better they like us'.

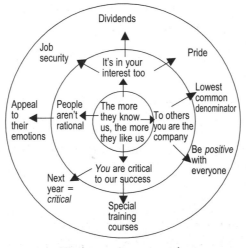

Mind mapping a speech

At this stage all that matters is that a total argument is seen to emerge.

How far does the complete picture radiate naturally from the central message? If a thought or a fact or sub-message does not radiate, it will be difficult to make the speech coherent and interesting. More importantly, it will not support your central message, so it has no place in the speech.

 GIVING IT A STRUCTURE

Without an appropriate structure a speech is no more than a collection of random thoughts. The next step is to re-shape your material to make it meaningful to your listeners.

No audience gives any speaker a grant of immunity with respect to logic, organisation or comprehension.

There are three stages involved in speech structuring:

Transcribe each sub-message from your mind map onto a separate index card. Add the two or three key words to each card that will remind you of the facts you will need to support each sub-message.

Lighten the contents of each card with just enough well-chosen quotations, asides, anecdotes and personal observations to amuse, inform and satisfy the expectations of your audience. Just enough, not overkill.

Rearrange the cards until you come up with a structure that your listeners will find both acceptable and intelligible.

The order you choose could be chronological (procedure one before procedure two, cause before effect, stimulus before response, problem before solution, question before answer), geographical (the UK, Europe, USA, the World), or perhaps some other arrangement. The important thing is that it is **logical**.

④ **PREPARING YOUR SCRIPT**

The best talkers are those who are most natural. They are easy, fluent, friendly and amusing. No script for them. How could there be? They are talking only to us and basing what they say on our reactions are they go along. For most of us, however, that sort of performance is an aspiration rather than a description. Our tongues are not so honeyed and our words are less winged. We need a script.

But what sort of script? Cards? Notes? Speech written out in full? It's up to you. There is no right way of doing it. Here is a simple method favoured by many public speakers:

- **Write** the speech out in **full**.

- **Memorise** the opening and closing lines and **familiarise** yourself with the remainder of the speech.

- **Summarise** the speech on one card or one sheet of paper. Use **key words** to remind you of your **sequence** of sub-messages, persuasive facts and other supporting material like quotations, jokes and anecdotes, that will vary the texture of the speech and amuse, inform and satisfy your audience.

The main advantage of this method is that the speaker will not only be sure to cover everything they want to, but will also come across as a natural and spontaneous speaker who is not merely reciting a prepared speech.

Think carefully about what suits you best and evolve a personal style. Its very familiarity will, in time, become part of its usefulness.

MAKING WHAT MATTERS WORK FOR YOU

✓ Base your speech on one key message. Boil this down to **one sentence**. Put it on a yellow sticky note, and attach it to your computer monitor or desk. Everything you say, do or show should support this message.

✓ Mind map your speech to ensure that your central message, and any sub-messages, are supported by your most persuasive facts. Also use this mind map to ensure that you have **not** included any facts that do not support your central message, or any sub-messages.

✓ Re-shape your material to make it **acceptable** and **intelligible** to your audience.

✓ Prepare whatever kind of script suits you best.

3 Beginning and Ending

Think of your opening and closing lines as the verbal bookends of your speech. They must be constructed well enough to support and hold together everything that comes between them.

1 FINDING A CAPTIVATING OPENING

2 PROVIDING A ROUTE MAP

3 ENDING ON THE RIGHT NOTE

things that
really matter

How will you begin your speech? Should you go in loud and wake them up or creep up quietly and lure them into listening? The manner of your approach depends greatly upon the image that you wish to project and the objective of your speech.

Similarly, you have a wide choice of endings. You can round off a formal or business speech with a summary or repetition of your main points, maybe by demanding action based upon your words or by finishing on a visual display. At the end of a social speech, you can wish the Club or Society and its members good fortune in the future, repeat your thanks, quote their motto, raise another toast, or even recite a poem.

Whatever your choice of bookends, play around with your words until you are satisfied they will have *exactly* the effect you are seeking.

IS THIS YOU?

● I sometimes hear myself opening by apologising for even being there. ● My openings and endings are very unimaginative, usually I just start with, 'Good morning, ladies and gentlemen', and finish with, 'Thank you'. ● My introductions are too wordy. ● I find myself repeatedly announcing the end, which never seems to come. ● My speeches just seem to fizzle out.

① FINDING A CAPTIVATING OPENING

As they tell their speakers at Shell, if you don't strike oil within two minutes, stop boring. It is essential to start well. Successful communicators often ponder, consciously and subconsciously, for days over their opening words. Allow yourself plenty of time to find a captivating opening.

A captivating opening is one that:

- Creates **excitement**, **positive feelings** and **impact**.

- Convinces the audience that you **know your subject** and that you are in **control of your material**.

- Demonstrates your awareness of your **audience's needs, expectations, composition** and **interests.**

The first three sentences of a speech set the course for success or failure: a good start points towards plain sailing, a bad one makes you sail against the wind.

The opening of a speech must be **appropriate** given your **principal objective** and the **nature of the audience**. It should also be **in tune with the rest of the speech**. Every speech is different and every audience is different. What sort of initial impression do you want to make? What are you trying to achieve?

Below you will find a selection of tried and tested

openings – or hooks, as entertainers call them – that will help you achieve your principal objective. Each of these openings can be **adapted** and **personalised** to help you begin on just the right note.

Initial benefit promise: The IBP is a classic technique for hooking an audience. It stresses maximum gain for minimum effort. Tell them what's in it for them: 'Would you like to add ten quality years to your life? Then think twice before reaching for that saltcellar. I'm Pat Smith and I'm going to share with you a few little secrets that can add those years to your life.'

Only three points. Most speeches are far too long. Audiences are grateful to any speaker who tells them, in the first few sentences, that this speech will contain no more than three important points. Consciously simplify complicated processes. Delight your audience with straightforward concepts and your efforts will be rewarded: 'Innovation consists of only three parts: defining the problem, searching for ideas, and practical implementation.'

Story or quotation. Some of the finest speechmakers like to open with a story or quotation which illustrates their purpose and, if possible, their point. If chosen carefully, a good opening will illustrate your topic or indicate exactly where you stand on the subject. It need not necessarily be funny; it could well grab the attention in other ways: 'Oscar Wilde said there is only one thing in this world worse than being talked about – and that is *not* being talked about. Today we launch a PR campaign that Oscar would have been proud of.'

Make sure your opening is appropriate to your objective. Appropriateness is the key to effectiveness.

Striking image. Sometimes you have to shake people up when trying to activate an apathetic audience or when dealing with difficult issues. Spell out the implications of your message to your audience. Get the focus firmly onto them and away from you. Telling them that the opposition out there is tough is nothing like as powerful as creating a mental picture of the **implications** this has for **them**: 'Just picture it... the people working in the consummate company of the 21st century. They are active, agile and aware. They know how to harness the best of teams, techniques and technologies. They share a vision. They have a new mission for a New Millennium. Now... picture **competing** with this company.'

Controversial statement. If you are to command attention, especially in a large gathering, you need to be larger than life. Most openings benefit from a touch of drama. A provocative statement will focus attention and whet the appetite of your audience in the same way as a headline in a newspaper. Whether they agree or disagree, they are sure to listen: 'Our training shoes are made by underfed Indian children and marketed by overpaid American sports stars.'

Joke or one-liner. It is unusual to open a 'serious' speech with a joke, because it can set the wrong tone and the audience will expect more of the same throughout the entire presentation. A jokey opening is most appropriate for entertainment, such as a wedding speech: 'What can I say about Jim that hasn't already been said in open court?'

If your opening does not make an impact, you will lose your chance for immediate success. You only have one chance to make a good first impression.

Consider other ideas too. There are so many new, exciting

and unconventional openings. Look for a method that **fits your personality**. Then **test your opening** on a friend. Have you used just the right words, in the right order, with the right timing? If you can leave it out altogether and it's not a loss, look for a better one. Then **memorise** and **practise** it.

② PROVIDING A ROUTE MAP

Once you have hooked your audience with an appropriate and memorable opening, you should **set the scene** by clearly stating your **topic** and **theme**, and perhaps the **reason** for the speech. Tell them if and when you will take **questions** and define the **limits** within which you will work. Otherwise some people may be thinking about aspects of the subject which concern them, but do not necessarily concern you.

Take the audience into your confidence. Tell them where you will be taking them and how long the journey will be.

Hook: 'The best way to predict the future is to create it. In today's competitive marketplace, it's not enough to build a better mousetrap. The world won't beat a path to your door. You must build them a motorway. The need for an overall marketing plan is acute...

Route map: ... and that plan has to have three parts: Research your market... Position yourself against your competitors... Then develop a promotional plan to highlight your uniqueness. During the next thirty minutes you will learn how to create your future...'

Then make a smooth transition into your first point, and before anyone knows it, they're committed to listening and the process has begun.

ENDING ON THE RIGHT NOTE

The conclusion of a speech is as big an opportunity as the opening, probably bigger. People remember longest the last thing they hear. A bad ending can ruin even the best speech; a good ending can salvage even a mediocre one. Yet the majority of speakers just fade away when they get to the end of their speeches.

Powerful speakers conserve a lot of energy and concern for the audience until the end and make the conclusion their dessert, something delicious with a memorable aftertaste.

The paradox is that you need to look backwards while at the same time pushing your audience forward to some sort of action. You need to bring the speech to a **climax**. You need to **sound** as if you have finished. But at the same time you want your listener to say 'You're right! I *will* do something about it.' Advertisers refer to this as the **target response** – what they want people to think, believe, feel or do as the result of what they have seen and heard.

The ending, like the opening, is too important to be left to the mercy of chance or the whim of the moment. It does not have to be long and complicated – indeed, it should not be – but it does have to be worked out in advance and well rehearsed. Don't say anything new. Don't simply paraphrase – which is to tread water. Remember your principal objective. **The conclusion must move your listener forward towards that outcome.**

A good ending should fulfil three purposes. It should:

- **Pull people together.** Produce the feeling that a common experience has been shared.

- **Reinforce your central message.** Create the image or thought you want to leave etched in your audience's mind.

- **Be a call to action.** Motivate them to think or do something differently or better, as the desired outcome requires.

Here are techniques that will help you achieve these objectives:

Learn your ending by heart. It is crucial to the effect of your entire speech and it must be perfect. This applies also to your opening, but **not** to the main body of your speech.

Make the sum more than the parts. Repeat your key points, but give them an extra dimension, such as a mnemonic, slogan, rhyme or even a quotation bringing the individual parts together. Synergy can take the argument that one, essential, insightful, step forward: 'Today we have covered five themes: **P**eople, **O**rganisation, **W**ork, **E**nergy and **R**espect. Put them all together and we have **POWER**.'

Change your style. Even the most lucid presentation can benefit from a dramatic, passionate ending, providing, of course, the drama and passion are seen as relevant to the argument. But drama and passion are only part of the performance. Eloquence demands appropriate language, a sense of poetry. Suddenly the importance, relevance and significance to the audience of what they have already heard becomes the more acute: 'Thank you for your hard work,... For your commitment, ...For your continued confidence and support. Together, we can trim our fat and still enjoy a profitable dessert.'

There are many ways to conclude a speech. However, remember that every speech needs its **own** ending, tailored to its content, participants, atmosphere, and to your desired outcome. The following list therefore is intended as no more than a broad spectrum of possibilities.

Challenge your audience. End on a positive, upbeat note. 'Now that I have shared my experiences with you, I ask every one of you to look deep inside your souls and ask yourself: Can we allow this situation to continue?'

Present a key statistic. People are generally turned off by too many facts and figures. However, one or two key statistics, held back until the end of a speech, can be highly effective, putting things into perspective. 'Let me close with some interesting figures. With Poland joining the EU, the current market of 10 million potential buyers of our products will grow to over 50 million. If we're serious about being a major player in that market, the time to aggressively expand our efforts is now.'

Bracket a speech. Bracketing provides the ultimate set of verbal bookends, because they match. The idea is to begin with an opening designed not only to grab an audience's attention at the start of a speech, but also – and at the same time – to set up a situation that can be exploited at the end. In this way you present your speech as a satisfying whole. The two brackets consist of a **set up** at the opening of the speech and a **pay off** at the end.

- **Set up:** 'Today, I confess that I've been daydreaming – both reminiscing about the past and predicting the future. We're celebrating a birthday, an anniversary. This company was founded exactly 30 years ago.'

- **Pay off:** 'At the end of my reminiscing, I've come to these conclusions: We have done much for this company, and this company has done much for us. You have a right to be proud as managers. Let's congratulate ourselves and them move on to the next 30 years.'

Adapt a good opening. In the first part of this chapter we discussed several approaches that also make good conclusions. However you finish, remember that your last remarks will linger in the mind a little more than what went before.

When you intend to take questions after a business presentation or following a motivational talk or persuasive speech you will need to prepare two closes: one to follow the body of your address, and one to serve as an encore after the Q&A session.

The conclusion, then, is the highlight of your speech, your final burst. Plan it well and practise it. The last sentence must come out perfectly. It is the last impression you leave with your audience.

MAKING WHAT MATTERS WORK FOR YOU

✓ Your opening is an opportunity. Grasp it. Devise a strong opening that's spot on for *this speech*, *this audience* and *you*. If the shoe doesn't fit, don't wear it. There are plenty of shoes that **do** fit.

✓ As soon as you have made them sit up and listen, take them into your confidence. Provide a simple route map and set out clearly any ground rules that will apply.

✓ End on the right note. Your final words should reinforce your message and motivate your audience to act or react as your desired outcome requires. If you don't tell them what you want them to do next, you miss a great opportunity to help achieve your principal objective. If necessary, prepare *two* closes, one to wrap up your speech and another to ensure *you* have the final word *after* question time.

4 Adding Flair and Style

Flair is imagination, excitement, empathy,
warmth and enthusiasm. Style is conveying a
message in a way that is both intelligible and
acceptable to an audience. Together, they provide
the sizzle in the sausage.

5

things that
really matter

1 **THINKING LIKE A LISTENER**

2 **WRITING LIKE A TALKER**

3 **CHOOSING YOUR WORDS CAREFULLY**

4 **USING IMAGERY FOR MAXIMUM IMPACT**

5 **REMEMBERING RHYTHM**

The moment you rise to talk to an audience, you step onto
a stage – metaphorically, and possibly literally. When you
open your mouth to speak to them, you enter a world
where corporate, scientific and technical terms must take a
back seat; where professional idioms must become
subservient to colourful, powerful, memorable English. The
more you accept this, the more successful you will be.

Having something worthwhile to say is *never* enough.
You need to know how to guide people towards given
goals. You need to know how to use words and images to
reach their hearts and win their minds.

Today people's expectations are high and their attention
spans are low. Merely to gain and hold an audience's
attention requires flair and style. If you want to keep them
interested, your speech must sparkle. So let's get polishing.

IS THIS YOU?

• *Quite frankly, I think my speeches are a bit dull. Sometimes I've suspected entire audiences of holding imaginary remote controls with their thumbs hovering over the off-button.* • *I would like to make my speeches more meaningful and relevant to a wider audience.* • *I find it difficult to convey abstract ideas effectively.* • *I know my subject well, but I'm not a good communicator.* • *I want to make my speeches memorable... and for the right reasons!*

① THINKING LIKE A LISTENER

Think about the best and worst speeches you have heard. How did you feel, as a listener? How did you respond to the speakers? Did you sit up and pay attention? Or were you annoyed, embarrassed and indignant? **Ask yourself** why you felt the way you did.

Put yourself in your audience's shoes. You need to think about the kinds of thing that will have a positive effect on them and stick in their memories.

Continually ask yourself: Will they be **interested** in this message? Will they **remember** my key points? Will they feel or think or do what I want them to? If you think like a listener you will engage their co-operation. Here are a few techniques that will help:

Tell stories. Everyone loves a story. If you can engage your audience with a *relevant* anecdote you are onto a winner. You will not only grab and hold their attention but also bring your speech to life by evoking strong images in the minds of listeners.

Matching your choice of anecdotes to the nature of the

audience is easy when the group is homogeneous – medical stories for doctors, religious anecdotes for the clergy, horsey tales for the gymkhana club. All your stories should have **a point to them**, they should **support your message** or at least one of your sub-messages.

Show pictures. People remember things much more easily if they are shown pictures. **People remember visual stimuli.** Can you recall the title of this book? Yet I am sure you can remember the colours of the cover.

Translate important words, ideas and concepts into pictures and make sure they see everything you want them to remember.

Most of what is shown during speeches and presentations is a waste of effort – at best. If a visual aid does not help the audience understand and remember the point you are making then replace it or leave it out.

Your visual aids should be **simple**, **original** and **memorable**. A picture is supposed to be worth a thousand words; it should not generate another thousand words.

Making a visual aid unique and memorable

Visual aids should be just that – *visual*. If you feel you must have words on your charts and slides, remember the tee-shirt test. Never use more words on a visual aid than you would on a tee-shirt.

- *Don't* overcomplicate things. Use only two different fonts, in two different point sizes.

- *Don't* highlight too much through *italics*, CAPITALS or **bold**. The more you emphasise, the less powerful each emphasis becomes.

- *Don't* use fancy borders that are more interesting than the words or images inside them.

Think how best to support your message and any sub-messages visually; don't waste time thinking about what use you can make of any sophisticated media to which you may have access.

Use emotion to good effect. C. S. Forrester reminds us that 'Words spoken from the full heart carry more weight than all the artifices of rhetoric.' While there may be no room for passion when your purpose is to **inform**, you should feel free to display strong personal feelings when you are attempting to **persuade** people. However, you must be genuine. False heartiness, cheap sincerity and – worst of all – crocodile tears will all be obvious to an audience.

Honour short attention spans. Psychologists have plotted how the attention of an audience varies throughout a speech. During a 40 minute presentation, attention starts high, drops gradually for about 10 minutes, then more steeply until it reaches its lowest point after about 30 minutes. Then it starts to rise steeply and remains high again for the last 5 minutes.

There are some important lessons to be learnt from this:

- Your most important points must be made at the **beginning** and at the **end**. In particular the last picture and last sentence or phrase will stay in the mind before new images and words are piled on top of them.

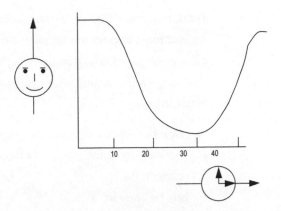

A typical audience attention curve

- Shorter sessions have a proportionately higher percentage of high attention time than longer sessions. Create 'mini-sessions' by breaking up the speech every two or three minutes with a textural variation, such as a visual aid, or say something that will draw some **response** from the audience – even applause!

- How many times have you been sorry that a presentation has reached a break? Now think how many times you have been glad. Enough said? Breaks are high points. Most public speakers provide far too few.

It is far better to have three 10 minute breaks than one half-hour break.

However, the audience's attention will **not** rise towards the end of a session unless they **know** that the end is nigh. So make sure that they do know (for example, 'Let me now take the last few minutes to re-cap.')

 WRITING LIKE A TALKER

Most people can write something to be read (known as

text), few can write something to be said (known as **script**).
Indeed most people are unaware that there is even a
difference. Every effective public speaker *must* recognise
that there are very important differences between text and
script, namely:

Text	Script
• is a journey at the reader's pace	• is a journey at the presenter's pace
• can be re-read, if necessary	• is heard once, and only once
• can be read in any order	• is heard in the order it is presented

*Written information should be easy to find. Spoken and visual
communication should be easy to remember.*

Spoken words are structured in **time**; written words are
structured in **space**. Putting across an argument in a purely
spoken form demands that both the speaker and the
listener are *always* at the same place in the argument.
Simultaneous comprehension is essential.

The order of words is different, too. We seem
subconsciously to understand the best order when we
speak, but we lose the knack when we write spoken text.
The lesson is clear: **Speak your words out loud before you
commit them to paper.** You will find that each element,
each phrase, each sentence, will be built from what has
gone before. Instinctively, you will take your listeners from
the *known* to the *unknown*; from the *general* to the
particular; from *agreement* to *disagreement*; from *present* to
future.

As you draft your speech, imagine you are talking to a
typical member of your audience. Ask yourself: Would I *say*

that to him or her, face to face? If the answer is 'no', don't *write* it either. Treat this person as an acquaintance, a neighbour. Look them in the eye, in your imagination, and make real contact with them as sharing our human situation.

Every communication is an opportunity to throw a bridge across a void. If you do this, your speeches will have more effect than you could ever have believed possible.

 CHOOSING YOUR WORDS CAREFULLY

The language of your speech should not be dictated by scientific, technical, industrial, statistical or other professional jargon. **Simplify** and **personalise** such material, even when addressing an audience of experts familiar with the specialist terms.

Break down the barriers which prevent you from sharing the thoughts and language and style of other professions. Speak in English, not jargon.

There is no specific and correct way to express thoughts. You have a choice of words, many with subtle variations of meaning and tone. You have a choice of word patterns that can create vivid pictures or touch the emotions and stay in people's minds.

Words are powerful. They conjure **images**, evoke **emotions** and trigger **responses** deep within us so we **react**, often without knowing why. So-called *warm* words make us feel secure and comfortable, while *cold* words leave us uneasy and unsure. Writer Henry James said the two most beautiful words in the English language are *summer afternoon*, because they evoke just the right emotions.

In speechmaking, we work backwards from Newton's Law that every action has an equal and opposite reaction. We decide the reaction we want and work back to the words that will produce them.

In the early days of instant coffee, advertisers got off to a bad start by stressing words like *quick*, *time-saving* and *efficient*. These are all words without warmth and feeling. Makers of fresh coffee fought back with warm, happy, appetising words like *aroma*, *fresh* and *tasty*. Makers of instant coffee soon learned the lesson and their product became *delicious*, *rich* and *satisfying*. Sales *blossomed*. The rest, as they say, is history.

Once you get into the habit of looking at the emotional colouring of words, as well as their meanings you will find yourself using the kind of language that puts listeners **at ease** and encourages them to **react more favourably** to your speeches and to you.

Use language well and people will perceive you to be as powerful as the message you convey.

Avoid weak, wishy-washy words. Replace uncertain phrases with strong, influential phrases:

Uncertain phrase	Influential phrase
● I think you should	● You should
● Can we discuss	● Let's discuss
● You may want to consider	● You should consider
● We really should try to improve	● We must improve
● I will try to answer that	● Here's the answer

Research has shown that audiences will always react favourably to the following twelve **impact words**:

● Discovery	● Easy
● Guarantee	● Health

- Love
- Proven
- Safety
- We

- Money
- Results
- Save
- You

Use these words and I guarantee you will discover how easy it is to get the results you want.

We and **You** are the most important words of all. When you talk to an internal audience, identify yourself with them. Talk about *our* competitors; the problems *we* face; the best way for *us* to go forward. When you address an external audience, make it abundantly clear that you are no more than a **catalyst**: *they* are the important people. They are the ones who must make the required changes in attitude, feelings or knowledge. Talk about *your* competitors; the problems *you* face; the best way for *you* to go forward.

You cannot stir your audience up if you do not address it directly. Remember the 5-1 rule: Every time you hear yourself saying I, try to follow it with five wes or with five yous.

 USING IMAGERY FOR MAXIMUM IMPACT

Imagery is the implanting of word pictures in listeners' minds to **illustrate, illuminate** and **embellish** a speaker's thoughts. Which of the two following rhetorical questions has the greater impact on you?

- 'Can we continue to allow so many hundreds of pedestrians to be killed on our roads every year?'

- 'How would you feel if the doorbell rang, you opened the door, and there, at your feet, lay the dead body of your child?'

No contest. The first question may make you **think**. The

second will make you **feel**. If you **tell** them they may **listen**; if you **show** them they will pay **attention**; if you **involve** them they will **react**.

One mental picture is worth a thousand words. An image can move the argument forward more cogently than pure reason.

Sensory details bring breadth and depth to your descriptions. Why? Because you want your audience to **believe** in your words, to feel they have left their seats for a few moments and are 'living' within the story. You want to turn passive listeners into **participants**. This can happen only if the world you describe has all the trappings of the real world. And the real world is a sensory experience: 'Norma led us around the dance floor to our table. She exuded odours of Avon soap, Woolworth's perfume and Juicy Fruit gum.'

Pepper your descriptions with sensory detail. It will bring your anecdotes to life like a shot of whisky in a cup of coffee.

 REMEMBERING RHYTHM

A good speech, like a good song, needs a regular beat. It should have a rhythm of its own; peaks, troughs, crescendos and a climax. It should have a lyrical quality that is music to an audience's ears.

Here are five simple devices that will add an almost magical, melodic quality to your speeches:

Link words. Have you noticed how entertainers, politicians and TV presenters move **easily** and **unobtrusively** from one topic to another? Like them, you can make your speech flow **smoothly** and **gracefully** from beginning to end by using link words like 'After all...', 'Nevertheless...', 'By the way...'.

- 'That was what the debtor situation was like in December. *Of course* things are different today...'
- 'Today we are the market leader. *Mind you*, three years ago it wasn't like that...'
- 'That's what a change of image can do for a company. *Okay*, how can we improve our image?'

The way a speaker keeps things flowing takes a little thought, but it's so worthwhile in its effect. How often have you winced at a clumsy transition or a hoary cliché: 'Which reminds me of the story of...'

The rule of three. Three is a magic number for speechmakers and communicators generally. Audiences love to hear speakers talk to the beat of three: 'Things have changed a lot over the last fifty years: From the Home Guard to home computers, from Vera Lynn to Vera Duckworth, from ration cards to scratchcards.'

Whenever possible present your ideas, thoughts or observations in groups of three words; three phrases; three sentences. Have you noticed how frequently the rule has been applied throughout this book, including in that last sentence? It doesn't sound quite so effective in twos and fours, but fives work almost as well.

Parallel sentences. Sentences that are parallel add a rhythmic beauty that helps an audience anticipate and follow equal ideas: 'To change is normal. Nothing is constant except change. Our interest rates change... Our clothes change... Our cars change... The face of our workforce changes... Our politics change... Our philosophies change... Even our cultures change. Change has become the status quo. Change is the only thing that's the same. That's normal.'

Alliteration. The repetition of sounds and syllables, usually at the beginning of words, can help create a mood or unite a passage of text. Alliteration can make your speeches special and spellbinding: 'A generation ago, we feared typhoid more than terrorists,... cholera more than crack,... and rickets more than redundancy.'

Repetition. If there is anything that is almost guaranteed to make an audience break out into spontaneous applause it is a repetition of strong, emotive words: 'We will fight, and fight, and fight again to save the Party we love!'

MAKING WHAT MATTERS WORK FOR YOU

✓ 'Think audience'. Put yourself in your audience's shoes. Think about the kinds of thing you could say and do that would have a positive effect on them.

✓ Don't be too concerned about the rules of grammar and syntax. Use **effective** language, not necessarily **correct** language. Write as you talk.

✓ Choose your words carefully. Corporate terms and exclusive jargon must take a back seat and professional idioms must become subservient to colourful, powerful, memorable English.

✓ Use language **imaginatively**. Allow your audience to do far more than just **listen** to your speech; allow it to **experience** it.

✓ Make sure that what you say **sounds** good. Your speech should have its own rhythm. Give it light and shade, valleys and peaks. Just as the varied rhythm and intensity of a fireworks display adds anticipation and excitement, so a landscape of valleys and peaks will keep an audience interested and involved. People need valleys before they can see peaks.

5 Getting the Delivery Right

Once you accept that you can approach even the most daunting public speaking engagement in exactly the same way as you approach informal communication, your apprehension will dwindle and your confidence will soar.

3

**things that
really matter**

1 **BEING CONVERSATIONAL**

2 **PROJECTING YOUR PERSONALITY**

3 **BEING HEARD**

These goals may sound glaringly obvious, yet few public speakers even consider them.

This chapter will **not** put you in a straight-jacket of artificial presentation techniques. You will not be told how to stand, how to gesticulate, how to look at people, how to talk. In everyday life you have no trouble with any of these skills, and the **combinations** in which you use them make up your personality. If you abandon everything that is natural to you and substitute 'acquired' mannerisms, you will come over as unnatural, awkward and insincere.

Whatever individual characteristics you have that are special to you should be nurtured and cultivated and worked on, for it is those personal and unique quirks of appearance, personality and expression that will make you out as a speaker with something different to offer. And that is never a bad thing.

IS THIS YOU?

● It's odd, but I feel I'm always very personable in everyday situations but not at all convincing or inspiring when I speak in public. ● It's like I'm standing aside from myself, listening to a voice that doesn't belong to me. It's very strange. ● As I stand up in front of an audience a kind of lead veil comes over me and all I can see is a close-up of myself. I hear my voice in a very loud way and every word I utter sounds awful. ● My voice dries up and it destroys all the natural flow, all the rhythms and any kind of creative spark or anecdote that might come in is destroyed. Terrible. ● I am aware that sometimes I put on an act which is influenced by my perception of how a person in my position should talk.

① BEING CONVERSATIONAL

When you are sitting leisurely, with family, friends or colleagues, your conversation will be naturally relaxed and chatty, because that is the language of easy communication. When you make a speech, the words and phrases you use should be more **considered, imaginative, creative** and **rhythmical** than your everyday language, yet the way you say them, the way you deliver your speech should remain unaffectedly **relaxed** and **chatty**.

All communication is personal, one-to-tone. It may be 'multi-personal' – it is never 'mass'. Talk to your audience just as you would to John and Jane Smith. What is the audience, after all, but a collection of John and Jane Smiths?

If you are different when you speak in public, you may be perceived as phoney, boring, or lacking in personality. As a result, people will not take to you and they certainly will not be convinced by, or remember, much of what you have to say.

Certainly you may need to speak a little louder or make other concessions to accommodate the needs of your audience, but, in essence, nothing in your delivery style should change. **You should be yourself made large.**

The key is to recognise what you are doing when you 'get it right' and achieve successful communication, be it formal or informal, business or social, and then stay with it.

You need to **recognise**, and then **capture** this **normal** style of communication and make it work for you, **naturally**, in any given situation, **regardless** of the stress level. When you walk into your office or a restaurant or a greengrocer's shop, you don't hover outside anxiously rehearsing how you will deliver your lines.

We all communicate each day without fear of failure. If you can understand how normal, relaxed, informal spoken communication works, you will be able to understand what you must do and keep on doing **when you speak in public**.

Talk to your audience as if you expected them to stand up in a moment and talk back to you. If they were to rise and ask you questions, your delivery would almost be sure to improve emphatically and at once.

Imagine, every now and then, that someone has asked you a question, and that you are repeating it. Say aloud, 'You ask how do I know this? I'll tell you.' That sort of thing will seem perfectly natural; it will break up and bring a variety to your phraseology; it will warm and humanise your manner of delivery.

Most of us are astonished the first time we hear our own voice. The resonant sounds we've heard in our heads seem thin and alien issuing from an audio or video player. **It**

doesn't matter. Think about some of our top personalities and most effective communicators: Jeremy Paxman, Kate Adie, the Dimblebys. None of these gifted talkers would win prizes at RADA. There is nothing of the mighty orator about any of them. All these famous and successful individuals stopped worrying about their voices long ago, if they ever did. They are each concerned with **putting across their ideas**. They speak to us with conviction, sincerity, urgency – and sometimes fun.

It doesn't matter whether speakers have accents which are unusual or even speech impediments, as long as people can understand them.

Paradoxically, an unusual accent or speech problem can often help to reinforce a message by making it seem real and natural.

From the moment you utter your famous first words you are testing different ways of catching people's attention and achieving what you want. All through your life you continue to build on those skills.

Your conversational abilities are far more practised than your literary abilities. Casual conversation is not constructed in a literary way. You do not always finish your sentences. You repeat yourself. You use ungrammatical constructions – **because you are obeying a different set of rules.**

During everyday casual conversation you are obeying the rules of effective spoken communication which have been learnt, instinctively, down the ages. Don't abandon these rules when you speak in public.

② **PROJECTING YOUR PERSONALITY**
Your personality is your greatest asset. It is personal chemistry that makes people want to do business with other

people. Very few of us, given the choice, will choose to work with someone we don't like or trust.

If you are already successful to any degree the chances are that you have a 'winning personality'. The challenge is to project it, not suppress it.

As an audience member, the worst feeling you can have is embarrassment for the person on stage. If you succeed in projecting your personality you will feel **comfortable** and **at ease**. If you feel comfortable, your audience will feel comfortable and become open, focused and receptive to your message.

You don't need to rehearse the body of your speech to be perfect, but you must be comfortable. Audiences don't expect you to be perfect, but they need you to be comfortable. **Mutual comfort is the key to assimilation and acceptance.**

Each speaker is **unique**; each has a **unique style**. What might be most effective for one person would be a disaster for another. Did Elvis, Sinatra and Johnny Rotten all sound the same singing *My Way*? Of course not. The artist makes the crucial difference. So, too, does the speaker.

Don't pretend to be Oprah, Montel, or even Jerry. Be yourself.

Think carefully about how you come across when you communicate effortlessly under everyday circumstances. Probably you will not have considered this before. It is an extremely useful exercise because it makes you appreciate what you must also do during your speeches. In particular think about two things:

The way you act. When a person talks informally, they probably sit or stand in a relaxed manner, breathing naturally, maintaining an appropriate level of eye contact, gesturing every now and then to reinforce their words, and smiling at intervals to establish and maintain rapport. Yet the moment this same person stands up to address an audience, they become nervous, distrust their innate powers of communication, and rely on a range of artificial presentation techniques.

The moment you are told to do something in a certain way you become conscious of what you should be doing naturally.

The way you look. Personal appearance has a major impact on how you are perceived by an audience. I would not presume to say any more about the way you dress or groom yourself, but would suggest you consider objectively what a powerful part of your assessment of others this is, and act appropriately.

Knowing that you should, 'be yourself' will stop you worrying about your 'performance', and allow you to concentrate on what really matters: message and outcome.

 BEING HEARD

If there is public address equipment available, find out how it works, get plenty of practice and then use it. Don't trust in luck and don't believe people who tell you to leave it all to them. **Accept personal responsibility.** You are the one who will look awkward if things go wrong.

You must be audible. If you are not, all else is lost.

If there is no sound-enhancing equipment, speak as **clearly** and as **loudly** as is necessary to be heard. If the only other person in the room was at the back, you would talk to them naturally, at the right level, without shouting or straining, by:

- keeping your head up
- opening your mouth wider than during normal speech
- using clearer consonants
- slowing down.

If you remember that you must be heard by the person who is farthest from you, however many other people may be in the room, you will make those same four natural adjustments to your delivery.

However, and contrary to conventional wisdom, if you make a conscious effort to talk more slowly simply because you are in front of an audience, regardless of whether the farthest listener is three metres or 30 metres away, your delivery will sound unnatural and artificial. It doesn't matter whether you talk quickly or slowly, as long as you are speaking at the **same rate** as you would to talk only to that person at the back.

MAKING WHAT MATTERS WORK FOR YOU

✓ Analyse the difference between your everyday, casual conversational style and the way you currently speak in public. Don't abandon the rules of effective spoken communication when you make a speech. Get back to basics, **get conversational.**

✓ Stop worrying about your 'performance'. Rehearse not to be perfect but to be **comfortable.** Concentrate on what really matters: message and outcome.

✓ Become **yourself made large** and make sure everyone present can **hear you.**

6 Taking Questions

Questions should be taken as an opportunity to interact with your audience. An effective question session can turn a monologue into a dialogue, a meeting of minds.

4

things that
really matter

1 **GETTING THE MOST OUT OF QUESTION TIME**

2 **ANTICIPATING AND PREPARING FOR QUESTIONS**

3 **MAINTAINING CONTROL OF YOUR AUDIENCE**

4 **DEALING WITH DIFFICULT QUESTIONS AND DIFFICULT QUESTIONERS**

As a public speaker you need to know how to handle questions. But if you suspect that someone is out to damage you it would be acceptable to offer to answer questions individually and informally after the speech.

Consider the purpose of the speech: if it is to entertain, welcome or say farewell, questions are superfluous to the occasion. The size of the audience is another factor. The larger the audience the more inhibiting it is to potential questioners. With audiences in the hundreds, questions are rarely a good idea.

But these are exceptions. Most speeches elicit questions. they are an integral part of the entire presentation. Audiences expect them as a right. Organisers demand them.

You should welcome questions as a method to encourage interaction and to take the focus away from yourself for a brief moment. Your aim is **to communicate**, and the word *communication* comes from the Latin *communicare*, which means *to share*.

IS THIS YOU?

• I am happy to give a speech, but find the prospect of having to answer questions quite terrifying. • Sometimes I find myself slipping into defensive mode which almost inevitably sets off a self-justifying ramble. • I find it difficult to avoid one or two questioners dominating proceedings. • I often become confrontational because I feel questioners are trying to catch me out or they just want to show how much they know. • My speeches usually end on an upbeat, positive note but the question sessions often just fizzle out and the whole thing ends in a bit of an anti-climax.

GETTING THE MOST OUT OF QUESTION TIME

An effective question session will have several positive outcomes, for both you and your audience:

- It will dramatically increase your audience's attention span and level of engagement.
- It will enhance your credibility and reputation.
- You will gauge the feeling of your audience towards your speech.
- Points of detail can be clarified.
- Arguments can be developed.

In order to get the most out of question time, you must approach it in the right frame of mind. It is particularly important to:

Have a positive attitude. If you approach questions as if your audience were trying to put you on the spot or catch you out, you are bound to become defensive. If, on the other hand, you approach questions as if your audience were paying you a compliment by showing an interest in your topic, the difference in your relationship with your audience will be tremendous.

Treat questioners with respect. Always try to imply that a question is insightful and relevant, but avoid overusing stock phrases such as 'Good question' or 'I'm glad you asked that', as these can make you sound patronising. If it becomes necessary either to clarify exactly what information the questioner desires or to check your understanding of the question, do so without ever embarrassing the individual: 'Let me re-phrase that a little; you seem to be asking...'

Continually reinforce your message. Don't go as far as the politician who ignores the interviewer's questions and simply repeats and repeats his tub-thumping message. Answer each question on its merits, but phrase your response in terms of its relevance to your **principal objective**. Try to **hook** your answer back to your **message**:

- 'Once again, I believe this emphasises our reliability.'

- 'And that's another example of us keeping to our word.'

- 'When we say a thing, we mean it.'

If you use the same turn of phrase over and over again, your credibility will suffer. Arm yourself with another two or three memorable ways of expressing your central message.

'Over the past five years we have lost:
- More customers than there were runners in the London Marathon.

- The equivalent of 13 customers for each person working here.

- Enough customers to populate (*a local village or suburb*).'

Always keep something in reserve for question time. This does *not* mean withholding a key element of your speech against the possibility of being asked an appropriate question. It *does* mean having **spare examples, illustrations, statistics, anecdotes, slides** or **expert opinion** which echo an argument or better still play to your main points:

- 'When British Gas tried this method they found that...'

- 'This is a graph showing...'

- 'Professor Higgins has concluded that...'

② ANTICIPATING AND PREPARING FOR QUESTIONS

Try to anticipate likely questions. With a little thought, many questions can easily be predicted. Here are a few ways to jump start your thought processes:

Consider generic questions. There are certain generic questions that you should prepare a response for in almost every business setting:

Benefit questions
- What will we gain by doing this?

- What are the alternatives?

- What is the risk if we don't do this?

Action questions
- What steps should we take to implement your ideas?

- Who will take responsibility for this project?

- How long will it take?

Cost questions
- How much will this cost?

- When would this be paid?

- How much do alternatives cost?

In addition to predicting and preparing for such generic questions, it is possible to anticipate and even encourage questions likely to arise after any particular speech by:

Reviewing your audience analysis. Because you have already analysed the audience in some detail, this part of question anticipation is easy. What would a typical person from this audience be likely to ask? By analysing the audience you raise their natural biases in your mind and thus approach the topic from their point of view. By doing so you will be more likely to encourage the type of question you are prepared to answer.

Brainstorming. Having two or three other people with you in a room for 20 minutes brainstorming questions will yield a far greater percentage of anticipated questions than you could ever generate by yourself. To conduct such a session, first let your colleagues know the topic of the speech, the nature of your audience and what you hope to achieve.

Planting and otherwise encouraging questions. It is a perfectly legitimate tactic to plant questions in the audience. Prepare 'text-book' answers that reinforce your central message.

The ideal response to any question is to answer it well and relate it back to your main message and use it as a means of improving relations with your audience – all apparently spontaneously.

Tell your confederate to ask a question to start the ball rolling or to fill in any embarrassing pregnant silence. If the question session comes at the end of your slot, or just before a coffee break, set up a final question which you can answer with **authority**. Your audience's attention will be at a natural peak, anticipating a change of stimulus, and so you can lodge in their alert minds a strong and positive impression of your competence, and of your main message.

③ MAINTAINING CONTROL OF YOUR AUDIENCE

Make the ground rules crystal clear immediately after your introductory remarks. **Set the boundaries**. 'I will be pleased to answer questions for up to five minutes after the presentation. I'm afraid we can't discuss X because of the pending litigation and we'll have to avoid the issues of Y and Z for security reasons.' Such comments at the outset set the stage for your control of what is to follow.

How you conduct the question period can be one of the most significant factors in the success or failure of your speech. Handled properly, question time can underline your authority.

There are a number of stages that should be followed if control is to be established and maintained:

Change gear. Relax. Take a seat. Say, 'Now let's pause for a few moments while I get my breath back and you think about what questions you might want to ask'.

Pay close attention to the question, and signal courteous interest. Pause, and let them see you are thinking about the answer. There are good reasons for doing so:

- It restrains you from making a hasty statement that may not address the question.

- It allows time to formulate a succinct reply.

- It allows the audience to see you are formulating a

thoughtful response.

- It gives value to the question, and to the questioner, by showing that thought is required before answering.

Repeat or paraphrase the question. The advantages of doing this are that:

- It allows the rest of the audience to hear the question.

- It ensures you are going to answer the question posed.

- It allows you time to think about your response.

- It is a useful way to neutralise pejorative questions: 'Why don't you stop polluting our environment?' becomes 'So you are asking how we can avoid pollution.'

However, avoid repeating a question as a matter of course at a small, informal meeting. It will make you sound like a parrot.

Embrace the question. 'That's an interesting angle', 'Yes, we should explore that further'.

Respond directly to the questioner, but also involve the whole audience. Say, 'We can see, can't we, why Dr Black has asked that question'.

Confirm that the questioner is satisfied with your response. 'Does that answer your question?'

You can tell a great deal about how an audience generally views your replies to their questions by watching their body language. They will nod their heads when they agree with you and frown, look away or shake their heads when they disagree. **Watch your audience attentively**, and try to **understand** what they are thinking. Do they agree or disagree? Are they interested or bored?

If body language is negative, you still have a chance to

have another go. Explain the point again, but this time make a particular effort to be clear and concise. Give an example or two, if it helps. If they continue to look uncertain, say: 'I see you remain unconvinced. Would someone be willing to voice the reasons for their doubts?'

Don't let your session limp to a close after the last question. Retain control. Say, 'I have time for one or two more questions'. This allows you to **end on a positive note**. For example, if you are asked a weak or inappropriate question or if you answer a good question poorly, you can simply take another. If, on the other hand, you do an exceptional job, you may want to look at your watch and say, 'I've taken enough of your time already. I think we should draw to a close now. I hope you found this afternoon useful.'

When you make a business presentation or deliver a motivational talk or persuasive speech, reserve the right to have the last word. Leave the audience with your final thoughts, not someone else's.

Once you have answered what *you* have decided shall be the final question, say: 'Perhaps I could now make a few final concluding comments before we close.' End the day's proceedings with your **second** prepared closing remarks – that pithy quote or challenging question that will leave your audience charged up and ready to act.

④ DEALING WITH DIFFICULT QUESTIONS AND DIFFICULT QUESTIONERS

This is not necessarily the same as *answering* difficult questions and difficult questioners. Learn from politicians; sometimes it's best not to even attempt an answer. There are certain questions that may be difficult to answer or may divert you from your message if they are not handled properly. Similarly, there may be individuals in the audience with a personal agenda that may not contribute to your objective. You must develop appropriate skills to deal with such people who attempt to use *your* question time for *their* own purposes.

Options for dealing with difficult questions. It is possible to handle any question without becoming aggressive or submissive. You could:

- Answer the question.
- Refuse to answer (explain why).
- Say you don't know, but will find out and let them know.
- Hold it for a moment until you have finished making a point.
- Promise to deal with it privately later.
- Refer it to an expert colleague.
- Throw it back to the person who asked it.
- Throw it to another member of the audience.
- Put it up for general discussion.

Here are some of the more 'challenging' characters you are likely to encounter, together with some suggestions on how you should react and respond to them:

Mrs Arguer. Don't get into an argument. She probably seeks recognition. Give it and then get on with your question period: 'You've raised some interesting points. I'd like to take time to explore them with you later.'

Ms Hostile. Try to answer patiently – *once*: 'Perhaps there has been a misunderstanding. Let me try to clarify the situation...' If the hostility continues, recognise it as such, use the power of the group to your advantage, saying: 'I don't think I'm able to satisfy you on that right now. Perhaps we can get together and talk it out later. Now we must move on...'

Mr Dominator. Don't allow him to take over. Remember *your* objective. Be polite but assertive: 'May we have your question please?'

Mrs Enemy. Emphasise points of agreement and minimise differences, or frankly ask that personalities be left out of it.

Miss Mistaken. She's wrong, but just can't or won't see it: 'That's one way of looking at it, but how can we reconcile that with... (state the correct point)?' Use the opportunity to explain your argument once again, from a slightly different angle.

Mr Show Off. His real motive is to show his colleagues how well informed he is. Don't be afraid to tell him how clever he is. Prolonged discussion offers no benefits. The quicker you can get off the subject the better. 'You're right, of course. I was talking about the German sweetmeat market in general, not their German market for marsh mallows, which obviously you know more about than I do.'

Mrs Tester. She intended to publicly probe your knowledge and experience. The golden rule is not to bluff or to try to excuse your ignorance. If you don't know, promise to find out for the questioner – and keep your promise.

But don't get paranoid. Questions will usually flow from the start and most will be honest and straightforward.

MAKING WHAT REALLY MATTERS WORK FOR YOU

✓ Treat question time as an integral part of your presentation. Recognise the potential benefits it offers both to you and your audience. Take a positive approach, treat them with respect and use the opportunity to continually reinforce your message.

✓ Anticipate the kinds of questions likely to be asked and prepare convincing answers to them.

✓ Maintain control of proceedings. Set the boundaries. If necessary, reserve the right to have a final word **after** question time. **Listen** to your audience's verbal language and **watch** their body language. Use question time as an opportunity to remove any doubts they may be expressing about your message.

✓ Be prepared to encounter difficult questions and difficult questioners but conduct the session with the right, positive frame of mind. Remember that the vast majority of questions and questioners are simply and innocently seeking facts and opinions.

Putting it into Practice

1 Be sure to learn the essentials

- Set out the principal objective of your speech in one sentence.

- Find out all you need to know about your audience.

- Decide what is most likely to move this audience to do what you want them to do.

2 Now create your speech

- Focus on the central message of your speech.

- Mind map your speech to ensure that your central message is supported by your most persuasive facts.

- Structure your speech so that it is meaningful to your listeners.

- Choose a way of preparing your script that makes you feel comfortable and confident.

3 Plan your beginning and ending

- Remember – it is essential to start well. The first three sentences can determine success or failure.

- Provide a route map. State your topic and theme and perhaps the reason for your speech.

- Plan your ending well. It is the highlight of the speech and the last impression you leave with your audience.

4 Add flair and style to hold your audience's attention

- Think like a listener. What will have a positive effect on your audience, so that they remember your key points?

- Imagine you are talking to a typical member of your audience when you are writing your speech.

- Choose your words carefully. Speak in English, not jargon.

- Use imagery to bring your speech to life.

- Make sure your speech has rhythm to keep the audience interested and involved.

5 Make sure you get the delivery right

- Talk to your audience as if you were having a conversation with them.

- Project your personality. It's your greatest asset.

- Speak clearly and as loudly as necessary.

6 Prepare to handle questions

- Use questions as an opportunity to reinforce your message.

- Anticipate questions and prepare 'text-book' answers.

- Maintain control of your audience by setting the boundaries.

- Be prepared to answer difficult questions with a positive frame of mind.